Uninvited
MEMORIES

DR. AUDREYANN MOSES

Earl Grey Chronicles

Uninvited

Memories

DR. AUDREYANN MOSES

OTHER BOOKS BY DR. MOSES

Kelly Crews Publishing:

Saved by Grace: Walking Through Affliction Into God's Deliverance (2017)

Voice of Truth Publishing

RITES OF PASSAGE: Does It Give American Black Youths the "Right To Pass?" (2010)

Written by AudreyAnn C Moses, PhD (Assisted by Kenneth Nyamayaro Mufuka, PhD)

Dedication

This book is dedicated to love lost and the

moment you realize you will be okay.

"A man may love for a season,

but Jesus loves always and forever." (acm)

"To everything there is a season, and a time under the

heaven... a time to weep and a time to laugh..."

(Ecclesiastes 3:1, 4a)

Acknowledgements

I would like to thank all of the wonderful people that God put in my life, specifically to help me write. I'd like to thank my creative writing professor and author, Sheri Reynolds who initiated the original formatting of Earl Grey as a homework assignment at Old Dominion University in 1999. Thank you, Valerie Baty who painstakingly read a draft full of my voice, with many errors, and turned it into my voice in English.

And, thank YOU for trusting that "Earl Grey: Uninvited Memories" is worth the time to read.

Enjoy!

TABLE OF CONTENTS

Preface

Earl Grey

I have always enjoyed a cup of tea after a long or short day. My favorite, of the varieties in my tea box, is Earl Grey. I prefer it hot with cream and honey. There is a little tea room I enjoy going to, they know what I like.

I was introduced to Earl Grey while stationed in Washington DC by the "at that time", love of my life. He found it in a novelty shop where the clerk told him it was romantic. That's all he needed to know. He bought the tea because he loved me and thought it would make me happy. I drank it because I loved him and because it was really good.

Earl Grey has been around since the 1800s in one form or another. Many tea companies now manufacture it, with their own twist to make it unique. Regardless of the manufacturer, the most important lure to Earl Grey is its unique flavor, and its calming effect, which is very effective on a high anxiety or extremely depressive day, as well as, several other emotional and medicinal attributes.

Even though the love that brought Earl Grey into my life is forever gone, I still enjoy my cup of tea everyday, winter or summer; and even though it can be drank hot or cold, straight or with lemon, cream, sugar, honey etc... I still

prefer it hot, with cream and honey.

Try it, you will love it.

Uninvited Memories

CHAPTER ONE

September 14th, 1999

05:55

I'm a radio girl. I prefer it to television. It's the last man-made sound I hear before I go to sleep and the first sound I hear in the morning. I absolutely hate ringing alarm clocks. That gawd-awful noise they make jerking you out of sleep and into a major migraine first thing in the morning. Whoever created that noise was sadistic. My clock-radio is quietly set on the classical station. This particular station's morning selection is soft classical and is very soothing. Somewhere between asleep and awake I heard the soft music. This morning they are featuring flutists. I love the way flutes sing, soft and smooth, like the feeling you get when you think of prefect love. If Tracy were home, this would certainly be the perfect time for enjoying early in the morning lovemaking. But, he is with his real wife... the one that's allowed to call him in

12

the middle of the night and demand his attention, regardless of where he is or what he's doing. I know her well; her name is United States Navy. She is so demanding and he loves her unconditionally. Actually, so do I, which is why the Navy was my husband for 22 ½ years and why I will be loyal until death do us part. Ha! Talk about an alternative lifestyle!

The radio comes on the same time every morning, 5:55 a.m. My sons, with their own way of waking up in the morning, think I'm nuts for setting it for 5:55. I remind them that for all those years the Navy entrusted me with ships and secrets, I think I'm capable of setting my radio to the time that suits me. At 5:56 the Writer's Almanac comes on. The commentator talks about famous birthdays and events in the literary world and he reads a poem every morning. At 6:00 am, there are a few moments of news and weather or traffic and then it's time to get up. So, I have a plan, even if it only makes sense to me.

While lying there, thinking about soothing music and love-making my memory dials turns all the way back to 1974. WOW!

CHAPTER TWO

New Year's Eve
December 31ˢᵗ, 1973

"Hey Diary" - - can you believe we live in DC." I checked into my first duty station at the Washington Navy Yard in Washington DC on November 25, 1973. When I stepped through the door "he" was standing there. I'm dusting snow from my shoes when I looked up. What welcomed me is the most beautiful smile I've seen all day. "Petty Officer Michael Flores, at your service!" He held out his hand, and after a moment of not breathing, I took his hand and said "Umm, hello, I'm Natalee, I mean Seaman..." He interrupted me, "Welcome aboard. Here's your badge, wear it at all times while you are in this building." I asked, "What happens if I forget?" His smile went away. He said, "Marines will surround you with guns aimed to kill." With a

15

little crinkled nosed frown, I said, "Thank you very much, I will certainly keep that in mind."

All new personnel, military or civilian, are assigned an escort on the day they arrive because the building is a secure facility and no one can walk about on their own until their security clearance is finalized. Petty Officer Flores was my escort. He escorted me through the building explained a few things along the way to the personnel office. His job was to make sure I didn't get lost and end up in the wrong place, surrounded by those Marines with guns. He was very kind and answered all of the "why come" questions I was allowed to know the answers to. To top it all off, he is so "oh-my-goodness-it's-hard-to-breathe-while-looking-at-him" handsome! He is almond completion, soft black curly hair and beautiful brown eyes. I asked as many dumb "new-girl" questions as I could think of so that I would be able to hang out with him just a little while longer.

I noticed that everyone, officer and enlisted, had a great respect for Petty Officer Flores. He is the supervisor for the computer labs, which is amazing to me because, although we learned about them in college, I've never seen a computer. My job is in the personnel records office and I am not allowed in his section of the building yet, but maybe one day I'll get to see these giant machines that supposedly run the entire command. I am just amazed there is a group of people here who know everything about computers and have control of the entire command in their hands, because if the computers stopped working, work stopped everywhere.

February 13ᵗʰ, 1974

"Hey "Diary - - you will never guest what happened today." Petty Office Flores came to my office to check on me. He knew the Marines had not killed me, so he wanted to make sure I wasn't totally stressed out already. I was surprised because I didn't think he remembered me. He is higher rank and eight years older than me. Basically, I'm a child under him. When he walked in I kept my professional face on; but, underneath I was all over the place and enjoying looking at 'Mr. G2 Navy!'

I thought he needed paperwork for something, so you can imagine my surprise when he asked me if I wanted to go to lunch with him and some of the other sailors from his department. It is someone's birthday or something and they are going to celebrate. What was funny, when he asked me if I wanted to go to lunch with him, I looked at my Chief for acknowledgement that he and his friends were "safe?" With a grin, my Chief assured me it was okay and to enjoy. I was glad because I really wanted to be with Michael; I mean for lunch with him and his friends, of course. I had a wonderful time and I met sailors from the "technical" side of the command. They are very interesting people. I was quite impressed with them. Petty Officer Flores held the doors, pushed my chair under the table and had me wait for him to fetch the car. I have not seen such treatment since I left home. I thought only southern parents taught their young men how to be gentlemen. I thanked him for a wonderful lunch.

18

I went to my office...he went to his computers I'm feeling grown-up. I'm happy!

May 23rd, 1974

"Diary - today was a good day." My supervisor is very impressed with my clerical skills, which is great considering I arrived with an associate's degree in secretarial science and I am currently working on my bachelor's degree in adult education.

Michael and I go out quite often, always with friends. There is always a house or barracks party or we all meet at the club on base. I have not been to a club off base yet. Not in a hurry. I like the security of our little on base club.

August 7th, 1974

Today Michael came to my office, but he was not his usual "geeky comic relief self" making sure I wasn't starving, locked out of my keyboard or something. He sat down at my desk but didn't say anything. So, I said, "Cat got your tongue, Petty Officer Flores?" He smiled that smile of his and asked me out for dinner tomorrow night, on a "real date" — just us. I didn't say anything for a moment, and then he said, "Cat got your tongue, Petty Officer Clarkson?" I smiled and said, "What time will you be picking me up?"

August 9th, 1974

He picked me up from the barracks, took me to a very nice restaurant and to the movies; something I wasn't really accustomed to since my faith frowns heavily upon movie going — such a heathen activity. We talked for hours about nothing and about everything. He was surprised that I completed two years of college and that the closest I'd ever been to a computer was my electric typewriter and watching them on TV, giant machines the size of the room. He thought that was very comical.

Needless to say, that was the first of many dates. He and I spent quite a bit of our free time together. He taught me all about the Navy, Washington DC, Maryland and Virginia. He treated me like a queen; and he taught me about love, something I definitely had not experienced, for real, before.

New Year's Eve
December 31st, 1974

Today is Michael and my first New Year's Eve. We went to the Iwo Jima Memorial for the U. S. Marine Corps Band Holiday Concert. He was very quiet and seemed a little sad. He finally said that it was the fifth anniversary of the death of his dad, who died in Vietnam. His dad was a Marine, so he would come to the memorial to honor him and when he needed to sort out things in his head and in his spirit. The Marine concerts are always awesome.

April 19th, 1975

21

Today is Michael's birthday. We went to Haines Point Park. There was a jazz band playing, which went well with our sunset picnic. We had a wonderful evening. On the way home, he told me we would not be together much longer. He said he will be transferring soon and leaving DC in a few months. I was devastated, until he said we are not meant to be a "forever after" kind of love. He said his job was to teach me how a real man, the right man for me, should treat me. He also wanted me to recognize when the wrong man came slithering around, trying to beguile me.

New Year's Eve
December 31st, 1975

"Dear Diary - you will never guess where we are right now!" New York City, NY for New Year's Eve! Can you believe it? I told Michael I've never been to New York EVER and so he brought me here. I am excited. We will be here for a week. We will go shopping and see a Broadway comedy play called "Murder Among Friends." When I called my parents to let them know where I was going for New Year's, they gave me a list of dos and don'ts and the phone number of EVERY relative we have within 30 miles of New York. I did call Uncle Willie and Aunt Catherine earlier today. We will hang out with them tomorrow. Right now, we are going to TIMES SQUARE! AAAHHH!!!

May 5th, 1976

"Dear Diary - I am very sad today." Michael is leaving for Italy. He flies out tomorrow morning. Even though I know I will spend the evening with him, I am already so sad. I have a headache. I have been crying since I woke up this morning — love-hurt tears. I have to get myself together because I'm still expected to show up for work — on time. I have to find my happy face.

November 2nd, 1976

"*Dear Diary — today was an exciting day.*" I'm in Hodges, South Carolina right now, sitting on the porch with a chilled glass of Lancers, reminiscing over the events of the last few months, actually of the last year. Yesterday was my birthday. I turned 22 years old. I've grown up a lot since joining the Navy and moving to Washington, DC. I have had many ups and downs. But all-in-all I have to say I have had a great life and a great career.

Today, however, is a big milestone in my life. Today I voted for the first time. I came home for my birthday and to vote for the very first time. I wanted to stand in line with my parents and cast my vote. I voted for Jimmy Carter. To be honest, I voted for Jimmy Carter because he is the Democratic candidate, because that's who my parents voted for and because he seems like a nice man. I don't know enough about politics to know if he is a good or bad politician. I heard enough "grown-ups" say don't vote for Gerald Ford, so I didn't. Time will tell. Ha! He can't be any worst than Mr. Nixon. My folks were so proud of me. My dad told me I was ten years old (1964) before he was "allowed" to vote without "harassment". My dad never misses an opportunity to vote. He says too many people died so that I would have this opportunity to vote today. I'm very proud of myself. <u>I VOTED!!!</u>

New Year's Eve
December 31st, 1976

"Happy New Year's Eve, Diary - I'm feeling a little lost." It feels unreal to have New Year's Eve without Michael? I don't even want to go out at all, but my girlfriends insisted. No one seems to understand that Michael was the only grown-up boyfriend I've ever had. For 19 years, I did everything with my family. Then I met Michael and started learning how to be a grown-up and do grown-up things and go to grown-up events. And now it's all over and I have to be grown-up all by myself. Anyway, my friends and I will be going to the Non-Commissioned Officer's (NCO) Club for a New Year's Eve Party. "Whoop-de-do!"

April 8th, 1977

Work is going well. I still love being in the Navy and I still love living near Washington DC. I could not ask for a better life. I've learned much about myself and the type of life I want to live. One thing I'm not doing well is Sabbath and church. I don't go, except of course, when I visit my family. I actually don't have a choice. Mom says be ready for church, so you do what, you get up out of the bed and get dressed and you go to church. And diary, you know my mom, don't even think about not taking something to wear to church. I'd be wearing her oldest 1960 dress. To be honest, there is no reason why I haven't found a church here; I'm just not ready to be a single young adult, committed to the church, especially in my faith. I'm sure that sounds quite heathen, but it's the truth.

The other thing I'm not doing well is men. I really feel like I need a PhD to understand men. Michael forgot to tell me there were no other men in the world like him. It's hard without him. I've gone out since he's been gone, but none of them are him. I still cry heart-hurt tears.

May 5th, 1977

"Diary - I had a great day at work." Unfortunately, I'm not allowed to say what we do at work, not even when the trash man comes around. Today we had a very exciting day because a very powerful person visited my command. We rolled out the red carpet. I was very excited. I was on the committee to plan the luncheon and the ceremony. We were very busy for the last couple weeks getting everything planned and in order. This was good for me because it didn't give me much time to think about Michael and it gave me a look at a bit of high-powered Navy politics. Quite interesting.

This day, last year, was the last time Michael and I were together. I always smile when I think of him. I used to tell him I think the only reason he took interest in me was because he could tell how naïve I was about men, relationships and especially the difference between sex and love. He would say that many men would want sex from me but not want to love me, all of me, the way I deserve. He became my "tutor"; again, something church folk would break their forehead frowning about! He introduced me to fine dining restaurants, picnics in the park and the Kennedy Center. He would send flowers to the barracks for me. My friends looked forward to the flowers just as much as I did. Ha! He spoiled me (and them) from end to end.

I remember returning from South Carolina on the train into Union Station in Washington, DC. As the train pulled into the station I was looking out of my window — at nothing in particular. Michael had to work, so I was not expecting him to pick me up. There was steam from the train and fog in the night. When I stepped off of the train, through the mist I could see Michael leaning against the pillars, smoking a cigarette with one foot propped against the pillars and one long stem red rose in his hand. He saw me and walked towards the door of the train. He threw the cigarette on the ground and pulled me to him and kissed me like I'd been gone for a year.

It was like a Humphrey Bogart movie. It was like that every time he saw me, as if he may never see me again, and he wanted the moment to be perfect. During the last several months before he left, we spent every available moment together. He taught me things about being in love I would never have learned from someone else, especially someone my own age.

As it is with the Navy, the day came for him to leave me forever and I knew that I would never see him again. I miss him so much. He's been gone a year and I still feel the sadness of the day he left and of never seeing him again. I wonder if he still feels the sadness.

There are times when I can still feel him, smell him or dream about him, all of which is getting old because I can't find room in my spirit to give to someone else. I would listen to "One Last Bell to Answer" by the Fifth Dimensions and on most nights, cry myself to sleep. No one is good enough ...no one is Michael. I've tried dating, but none can begin to measure up to him. They are too young and too anxious to get where they don't deserve to be. A year ago I wasn't so sure if

I would survive being without Michael, but I know I will survive and that I will be fine. Well, that is, if I survive this night out with the girls. The last time they tried to cheer me up, I got drunk off of Zinfandel and had to leave my car at the club until the next day. They are trying their best to "help" me meet someone. I am not trying to meet anyone; I won't ever meet anyone to replace Petty Officer First Class Michael Flores — ever again.

Ok my dearest Diary - I didn't mean to write a book, but I had to get it all out and you are the only one that listens without butting in with your two cents worth. So now I'm putting on my happy face and going to the club to celebrate something fun with my friends. YIPPEE!!

CHAPTER THREE

September 14ᵗʰ, 1999

6:30 A.M.

It is Tuesday and I am so glad, because I couldn't stand it if it were Monday again. The only good thing about yesterday was the glimpse of that "kool-drink-of-6'3, 190-lb. brown-sugar and cinnamon - Mr" I saw in front of the coffee shop at the train station yesterday. MER-CEE!! I could not see him clearly, partially because of the crowd, and mainly because I'm only 5'2" and about as blind as a bat. However, I'm having the same "feeling" as yesterday, that there was something familiar about him. I don't remember seeing him in the coffee shop before and I go there almost every morning to wait for the train. A Temptations' song comes to mind, "just my imagination once again... running away with me." Right now, I need to focus more on getting out of this

31

bed and less on my imagination. I have too much going on at work to miss my train.

My not-so-good angel: "Hmmm...but a glimpse of him would certainly help start my day off right..."

My good angel: "Ignore her! You already have a really good man who is insane crazy about you! STOP TRIPPING AND GET DRESSED!"

Me: "Yes Ma'am Drill Sergeant!" Hahahaha!

As usual, I'm staring into my closet trying to figure out what to wear. It used to make my ex-husband crazy that I very seldom decided what I would wear in advance. Between night and morning my clothes mood would always change. Humm...maybe that's why he left. It was so much easier when I was in the Navy. "Which Khaki uniform should I wear today... pants or skirt...flats or heels?" Since retiring three years ago, I have acquired a wardrobe somewhat acceptable by corporate America, but today I couldn't decide. I finally decided on a dress. It's an olive green, to the knee, sleeveless a-line dress, with a short waist jacket. It compliments my

45-year-old, size 12 figure, perfectly. I looked in the mirror and smiled at the image facing me...Perfect! Walking really does work! If Mr. Mystery Man is near the coffee shop today, he won't have any choice but to notice me!

I ride the train to work because I hate driving in the city. I work in downtown Atlanta. Driving in downtown Atlanta is reserved for insane people. The train ride gives me an opportunity to meditate, talk to God about the issues of this new day, read my devotion or Sabbath School Lesson or some other book. I get to learn something about my God and prepare myself mentally and emotionally for the day, before I walk into my office. The train ride home gives me an opportunity to thank God for His assistance throughout the day and to read something fun, like a great mystery novel. It is already a beautiful Atlanta day. The sun is out and the breeze is perfect for the two-block walk from my house to the train station.

I love walking, watching people rush to open their shops and prepare for customers. My mind went back to 1977 - Fort Myers Army Base, Arlington, Virginia. We both lived in the enlisted barracks. We would meet each other early and go walking before breakfast. He would always try to make me jog. I told him "jogging was for people trying to die early!" Wow! that was such a long time ago, when life was simpler and I had finally allowed myself to think that love would last forever. I have an odd feeling that today is not going to be a typical Tuesday. Seeing Mr. Mystery Man triggered some old memories and feelings. Feelings I locked in that drawer over there hidden behind that brick wall. I left the key in the drawer and sealed the wall, so I wouldn't be tempted to look in it. Feelings I don't want conjured up again – ever. If this stranger can make me think of a life long ago buried, I don't want to know him outside of my imagination. I fear that in reality, he would be a devastation in my life...definite devastation.

I arrive at the coffee shop for my usual breakfast of a croissant and hot tea, Earl Grey with cream and honey. Earl Grey tea has been my beverage of choice for many years. He bought some from a specialty store because the sales lady told him it had a "romantic" flavor. He was so proud of himself when he brought it to me. "Hmmm, I had forgotten about that." I wonder what would have become of us if his career had not become more important than us. Oh well, then was then and now is now. Then I was naive about life and love. Now, I am Dr. Natalee Morgan, retired United States Navy Chief Navy Counselor. I now work for The Honorable Constance Abraham, Congresswoman D-GA, as the Chief Investigator for the Military Equal Employment Opportunity Department for the State of Georgia.

I love this coffee shop, whose name is "The Coffee Shop." The waitresses know me, especially Sally. She and I have become good friends. She's usually working the early morning shift. She's 26, working her way through law school. It's great to hear her says, "Hey Nat, having the usual?!" We actually have a coffee shop family. Mr. Peterson pronounces my name "Na-`tal-lee." His family is Italian, and that's how they pronounced his mother's name. Mr. Peterson retired from the Air Force at age 38 after 20 years' service and then retired from the post office at age 65 after 27 years service. He never catches the train, just comes for early morning coffee and to read the paper. He lives across the street from me and before his wife died, I remember waving at them as they walked pass my house, with their dog, Mr. Tibbs, on their morning stroll. On Tuesday morning's their stroll included a stop at The Coffee Shop. He called it their Tuesday morning date. She passed away in the spring, but he continues to come to the coffee shop, now every morning instead of just on Tuesdays. He says it's his morning exercise, but I think it's because he misses having morning coffee with his wife. He loves talking about his daughter, the school teacher. In actuality, she holds a PhD in History and Philosophy and is the chair of the History Department at the university. He is so proud of his daughter, and she loves her dad, so, she lets him call her "the school teacher."

Jeanette, who pronounces her name Gee`nete because she is a promising jazz dancer, works downtown at this cute little bookstore. She is a beautiful young lady with medium length brown hair and long legs. I think she's a little too skinny, mainly because she refuses to eat a real meal. I've been to a couple of her shows and she is a good dancer. Still, I hint to her about going back to college to complete her studies…just in case. She says she'll look into it but she will be on Broadway someday. Maybe she'll send us tickets. Ha!

Pastor Jeffrey Bannister is the Family Ministries Pastor of a very large church in Atlanta. He is also a subject expert when it comes to matters dealing with religious liberty. I met him through his wife. She and I graduated from the same PhD program. I visit their church on occasion and I have had opportunities to confer with him regarding a couple cases involving religious issues for military members.

As I sit having my breakfast, I find it hard to concentrate on my reading. I try not to think about work during my quiet time. The coffee shop and the train ride are the only private time guaranteed to me during the day. I'm reading this morning's devotion, about fear and faith, for the second time, and I'm still clueless. So, I decided to switch my

routine and read Sheri Reynolds book "Bitterroot Landing."
Ophra Winfrey had Sherri's second book, "The Rapture of
Canaan" on her book club list, which I thoroughly enjoyed, but
Bitterroot Landing is my favorite. Unfortunately, I'm having
a hard time concentrating on my book because I keep thinking
about this case I received yesterday. Something about it really
nagged at me. We received a letter from the mother of a U.S.
Navy Second Class Petty Officer stationed aboard the USS
Greenwood Lake (AD-30). He works in the engineering
department on the ship. He told his mother he is being
harassed, by his shipmates because of his religious beliefs. The
harassment started after a new supervisor came onboard to work
in his department. The letter stated, her son felt he was not
getting support from his superiors against the harassers and
that his request for an officer candidate program was not being
acted upon. The final paragraph in her letter read, "I'm
writing this letter on my own. My son did not ask me to write
you. I know he will endure the harassment and mistreatment
until he is transferred or until something terrible happens. I

hope you will take care of this problem. My son is a good, Christian boy who loves the Navy and what he does. He should not have to put up with such foolishness, especially since his father is a retired 30- year Navy veteran and since my boy volunteered to defend this nation against enemies foreign and domestic AND had planned to retire, as his father did. Most importantly for you, Congresswoman Abraham, he is a registered voter for the State of Georgia. Thank you kindly for your service to the great state of Georgia, and, for your assistance in this matter. May God continue to bless you. "

I really do not like military religious cases. They are always because the faith of the individual is not "traditional" and therefore rubs against the grain of other military individuals and military structure. Nobody wins and the best we can hope for is a forced compromise. So, along with my other cases, I have been personally assigned to handle this case for two reasons: one, because of my navy background; and two, because the faith in question is the same as my faith. Once I have enough details, I will definitely be conferring with Pastor Bannister.

To get my mind off of the case, I began to watch the other people coming and going. To most people, of course, this coffee shop is just a stop along the way. I wonder if sitting here every morning calms their spirit as it does mine. My friends say I feel everything too deeply. My idea of a near perfect life is a relationship with Christ, a career I like, a few good friends and a relationship that is monogamous, fun, full of love, understanding, trust, communication, etc. I don't think that's too much to ask. Actually, I know it's not because I have all of that right now. I am blessed that, after all of these years since my divorce, I have a man in my life able to handle my "deepness." There was a time long ago when I thought I had found the one, but in the end, he could have handled me, he just wouldn't. His future was more important than our future.

I'm sure Mr. Mystery Man's coffee shop experience of yesterday is a forgotten memory for him and I need to make it a distant memory as well. Nevertheless, imaginative anticipation keeps lurking about in my stomach. It's actually quite sickening for a woman of my age to be daydreaming over love lost 20 plus years ago. There will be no fairy tale rekindled romance happening here.

CHAPTER FOUR

September 14th, 1999

8:00 A.M.

I am not so engrossed in thought that I cannot hear the screeching halt of a train; and recognize the little bell on the door as it jerks me back to reality and several people trample into the shop. As I force myself to focus on life in the present there seems to be a change in the aura of the room — literally. At this very moment everything looks blurry, as if a sheer curtain is being draped from the ceiling between me and the door. I closed my eyes for a second to clear my sight. I opened my eyes looking at the floor as a pair of soft grey leather shoes, barely covered with gray slacks, walks towards the counter. As I look up slowly I see his hand reach towards his back pocket. Hanging from his wrist was a gold and silver double linked chain with an anchor pendent on it. Oooo…Oh my goodness…I caught my breath and stopped myself from reaching out to touch his hand; because the bracelet is identical to the one I gave Scotty for his birthday, twenty-one years ago. When I bought it, I thought it was a one-of-a-kind, but I guess not. Instantly there were bodies between the grey slacks and me. I took a deep breath, shook my head just enough to feel my twists brushing against my ears. My goodness, this day is getting crazier by the moment.

My nerves are all frayed from the "sighting" yesterday and my memory jumping back and forth on my life line is not helping. Now I'm imagining things and copy-cat bracelets. My head is on the verge of a migraine. He could have been my life, but I reminded myself that all those years ago, the two years we were inseparable at Fort Myers, was not as important to him as his plans for his career. His words were "It's not that I don't love you, Nattie, but how could I pass up such a lucrative career opportunity...for this?" Thank you, Holy Spirit, recollecting that bit of repressed memory helps to bring me back to reality, back to 1999, where he does not exist. I have to admit, looking back, he did me a favor. I had a very rewarding navy career which put me in the direct path of my current position. I met a wonderful man and had a great marriage, for a season. Although the marriage didn't last, I have two very handsome, teenage sons as a result. My relationship with Christ is improving daily. My career is flourishing and I enjoy spending time with a real, southern gentleman sailor. In fact, he comes home from assignment tonight and we are going to Stone Mountain tomorrow. Another deep breath...I thought, "Thank you God for new memories and the wonderful life you have provided for me."

It was unusually crowded and noisy in the coffee shop, so I decided to wait outside since I couldn't concentrate, and my train would be in the terminal shortly. While attempting to clear my table, pick up my purse and briefcase, all at the same time, I turn towards the door and walk immediately into the grey slacks and sweater. He is standing directly in front of me, looking at me, as I look at him. The smile on his face grew into beautiful white teeth as his free arm reached for me. Before I could move I was enveloped between his arm and the

44

grey sweater. I can smell him...and feel his heart beating fiercely. At this moment, all of my senses are teaming together to focus on the voice I am hearing, this Melvin Franklin bass voice, in my ears. I can hear him whispering my name, Nattie! Nattie! Only he called me that, so I knew he was him and not a stranger or a hallucination. He is wearing Grey Flannel cologne. I introduced him to it as an alternative to Old Spice. He is saying something, but time and movement seem to be frozen for a moment. I can hear Mr. Peterson, "Sally who is this, he is not Tracy?" and I can hear Sally telling Mr. Peterson "I bet it's one of her old friends from when she was in the Navy."

As he dropped his arm I staggered just a bit, trying to catch my breath, as I look up at a very alive 6'3" figment of my imagination. "Nattie, I thought I saw you yesterday, but just figured it was my imagination. That's why I came back today, just in case." I had no idea you were living in Atlanta. Before I could say anything, Ms Commentator Sally is blurting out, "She saw you too, but she thought it was her imagination." I'm glaring at her with my "wait till I get you home" look! Like most "children" she is ignoring me. I introduce him to Sally so that she would close her mouth and to Mr. Peterson so that he won't call Atlanta's Finest or even worst, his "people."

I want to leave right now, go back home, get in my bed and stay there until tomorrow. My heart is beating so fast, I definitely have a serious migraine. I still have all of my stuff in my hands and I am just looking at him. I'm thinking to myself, "Holy Spirit did I ask you to actually bring him here...No I Did Not! I don't remember asking for that! In fact, Lord, I know I was perfectly okay imagining who my Mr. Mystery Man might be." As I hear my train pulling up, he asked, "Nattie, do you have to leave right now?" I laid my things on the table and sat down while he asked Sally to bring him a coffee. "God, why does he still look this good...why isn't he fat with brown teeth!" "I just want to know why he is here! What am I supposed to do now?"

I have not said anything to him yet because I am on the verge of tears. I know if I hear my voice I won't be able to hold them back. So, I just sit here in silence. And he sits there in silence, smiling and looking at me. This was the first time we have been in the presence of each other for over 20 years, except of course in my dreams. Maybe I'm still dreaming. Mr. Peterson's voice assured me that I am not dreaming. "Na'talee, will you be okay? You want I should stay here with you?" His voice is directed to me, but his eyes are piercing right through this stranger. I said, "No sir Mr. Peterson, I will be fine. Besides, Mr. Tibbs and Ms. Valerie will be standing at the door with their legs crossed, wondering why you are late getting home to take them out." He said okay, as he kissed me on the forehead while starring in the direction of my surprise guest, with an expression that clearly says, "If anything happens to her..." As he walked out he said good-bye to Sally and told her to call him if necessary. She said, "Yes sir Mr. Peterson."

Sally decided she should bring me another cup of tea, mainly so she can get a better look at this mystery man. He smiled as she said, "Nat, I think you can use another cup of Earl Grey." I nodded and said thank you. "You still drink Earl Grey?" he asked with a satisfied smile. I said "Yes." Then the questions started. "How have you been?" "Where have you been?" "What have you been doing?" How long did you stay in the Navy?" He keeps saying he can't believe he ran into me after all of these years. "Well", I said, "we certainly cannot catch up on 20 plus years in a couple minutes." As the words are coming out of my mouth, I am kicking myself because I don't want him to think I am the least bit interested in catching up. The trains are pulling in and I have to admit I was relieved. It was going to be a hectic day and I didn't need added stress. As I picked up my purse and things, he stands up and gives me his card. I frown as I read, "Headquarters, U.S. JAG Corps". Excellent, he made it. His goal was to be Navy JAG, good for him. However, my investigative antennas started twitching. Why is the Navy's

Judge Advocate General office in Atlanta? The air station is here, but there is nothing going on that would involve them, that I know of. When I get to the office I will definitely ask Nancy to see what she can find out. I will ask Tracy when he returns. Since he's the air station's head of security he should know. Scotty's voice pulled my brain back to him saying, "Page me PLEASE" as he walked out of the door. Hmmm, he looks just as good going out as he did coming in! I looked at Sally, shook my head and walked out the door to my train. "God, this is a distraction I don't need right now!"

As I sit on the train, I try to read, but I can't concentrate. As I just stare out the window, against my will, my mind went back to how I met Scotty...

July 16th, 1977

Diary - I know I have not written in a while. I'm a little depressed. Work is going great. I no longer work at the Washington Navy Yard. I'm working at the Navy Annex in Arlington, VA. It's not like I moved to another town or anything. I'm still in the Navy. I love working at the Navy Annex. I'm the Navy's equivalent of an executive secretary for one commander. Now I really get to use my two-year degree in secretarial science, especially my shorthand. I've been using it to transcribe almost anything I hear so that I don't forget this unique language. Now, I am using it every day. The one thing I absolutely love about my job is going to the Pentagon once or twice a week for one reason or another. That's exciting, walking around in the building where war begins and ends. I miss Michael but I'm not miserable anymore. YEA!!!

It's Saturday morning — Thank you God for the weekend! One of the joys of working at the Annex is that I have almost all of my weekends free. I plan to go to Haines Point Park this afternoon just to chill for the day. I've been trying to finish this Agatha Christi novel, "Ten Little Indians." I can sit by the water, read and watch people coming and going. It will be a pleasant afternoon. It's been a very busy, very hectic week and I'd just like to spend some time with me for a change. People don't understand I'm an

introvert (I learned that in my psychology class Ha! Ha!).
All the hustle and bustle drains me. I need some alone time to
rejuvenate myself.

Right now, I'm still in my room sitting by my window
watching one of the honor guard drill teams practice. The
Honor Guard is a segment of the Old Guard of the Army,
stationed at Fort Myers Army Base in Arlington, VA. They
are responsible for all of the ceremonial events that occur in
Washington DC and at the National Cemetery (which is
attached to Fort Myers). They are fabulous. I love watching
them. It is amazing how sharp they look even in their working
uniform. Don't get me wrong, I'm a sailor girl through and
through; there is no man more handsome than a sailor in dress
blue Crackerjacks and those thirteen buttons. There is no
comparison!

However, there is one soldier I look for when the honor
guard is practicing. He is their trainer. He is about six feet
tall, looks great in his working uniform and fabulous in his
dress uniform — oh my goodness!

I've seen him around base, but I haven't spoken to him. He was at the club New Year's Eve. Since we all live in the barracks, I'm sure he already has a girlfriend — one from each branch of the service. And with that thought I'm leaving for my adventure in the park.

July 17th, 1977

I had a wonderful time at the park yesterday. I actually finished my book. Of course, it wasn't all solitary. Haines Point Park is a popular hangout spot so, of course, eventually several friends showed up. And guess who was with them...my mystery drill soldier; AND he knew who I was! How does he know me? What a day! Gotta go right now, meeting the girls. We are going to Kings Dominion! Talk about him later.

August 15th, 1977

"Dear Diary - GUESS WHAT HAPPENED TODAY!!"

I was promoted to Personnelman Second Class. I was unofficially promoted in May — meaning I was doing the work without the pay! I am now a PAID team leader and supervisor. Another good thing happened this week - I finished junior year. I aced my finals and now I'm a Senior! YAY!!!!! Bachelor's of Arts — Adult Education here I come!

WOW, this is a double blessing. I can't wait to call my folks. They will be so proud of me. I wish I could tell Michael. I know he'd be very proud of me.

Two goals accomplished on the same day. Thank you, God!

New Year's Eve
December 31st, 1977

"WOW Diary - where have the days gone!" I can't believe the year will be over in a few hours. It seems like it flew by. I guess it's true when they say, "time flies when you're having fun and love."

I've been seeing someone for a few months. It's been nice. Michael was almost right. He said the right man will make me forget about him. Well, I won't ever forget him, but I certainly don't dream about him and pine over him anymore.

Scotty - real name Trevour Scott, United States Army Honor Guard. I could watch them perform all day. They are so dignified. As much as I love the Navy, I have to admit that the Old Guard is the best of all the services.

Anyway, Scotty and I have been seeing a lot of each other since we "formally" met in the park. It's been wonderful. This will be the best New Year's Eve celebration since Michael left.

CHAPTER FIVE

September 14th, 1999

10:00 A.M.

My calendar is full - four meetings and three scheduled clients. Nancy, my assistant, already filled the only vacant time slot on my schedule with a new appointment that had come in overnight and we always have at least two walk-ins a day. There is no time to think about Scotty today, however, the fact that the Navy's JAG Corp is in Atlanta bothered me. I told Nancy about running into him and when we were together at Fort Myers. Now he's a commissioned officer, a lawyer for the Navy JAG Corp and in Atlanta...Why? Nancy is making calls to see what she can find out; because this inquiring mind most definitely needs to know.

I told her how he and I parted. As she walked toward her office she just shook her head and said, "Men! Tell me again why we can't just kill them!" "Because, it's against the law!" I laughed and started reviewing files for my appointments. A mind is a terrible thing to waste, and right now I seem to be involuntarily wasting mine thinking about Scotty...again.

March 17ᵗʰ, 1978

"Diary - you know better than anyone how I feel about the Navy. Joining the Navy was the best thing I could have done for myself — EVER! I tell everyone the Navy saved my life... LITERALLY! I have met great friends and I really love my job. I could not have picked a more perfect career for myself. And then there's Scotty. He and I are a pair together. Scotty and I have done well in our careers. We have both been promoted and are in supervisory positions. He travels a lot in his job, so we are not under each other constantly, which is good because sometimes I need a break. And I have other goals, such as higher education, which is hard to pursue with a man underfoot all the time. Now that I work at the Annex and make more money, I have my own apartment and car — a 1977 Volkswagen Super Beetle. Also, since I'm not at Fort Myers as much, Scotty and I don't see each other every day anymore. Whenever he sees me he swoops me up in his massive arms and lifts me right up off the floor; he hugs me tight and tells me how he will never let me go. Well, we are still new, but it does sounds good!

I got promoted again today. I'm not making more money but I am working for the captain of our department — which comes with GREAT benefits, including travel because I go everywhere she goes. Yea!! Scotty's gonna hate that.

I see all around me that God is continually blessing me, even though I don't worship him like I should. He takes care of me and promotes me, although I'm not expecting it. He keeps me out of danger, even when it's my fault, and He obviously loves me. I really need to get myself together spiritually. My parents keep "bugging" me about going to church. My mom would remind me that I don't even sing anymore. I remember how much I loved singing, especially in

the choir. I guess, maybe, I should start thinking about,
thinking about looking for a church, maybe.

April 9th, 1978

"Diary - do you believe it's been a year since Scotty
and I have been together. WOW how time flies!" We have been
having a wonderful time, whenever we are both in town at the
same time.

For our anniversary we went to the movies to see
Superman and to dinner at Chesapeake Bay Seafood House —
MY FAVORITE! Their cinnamon rolls are to die for!

We were having a great time until Scotty wanted to
have this "where do we go from here" conversation, which I
really wasn't interested in having; however, as I listened I
began to realize the conversation was geared more towards his
career and less about us as a couple or my career. I'm not
really sure where he is going with this. He's acting a little
strange and I'm feeling like I need to start thinking about

protecting my emotions from him. Well, I shouldn't jump the gun...I guess.

May 15ᵗʰ, 1978

02:00 A.M.

"Diary — YES, I'm just getting home." This was the first chance we had to celebrate our "anniversary." Scotty took me to dinner and a play at the Kennedy Center. I had not been there since Michael. Then we walked around by the wharf for a little while. He still wanted to talk about his plans for his future. He wants to go to law school and eventually work for the Judge Advocate General; basically, he wants to be a military lawyer. I told him I think that's great if that's what he wants. I told him I wanted to work on a master's degree in counseling. I couldn't start until I knew where my next duty station would be located, which will preferably be overseas. If I start my studies now, my credits won't transfer

to another college. Again, I felt as if I was talking out loud in an empty room; as if my personal needs and my career goals were of no importance to him. I could sense the tension, so I changed the topic and we had a great evening. Now that I'm sitting here alone, thinking about the last few days and the conversation, I really think he is making plans, maybe without me. I guess I have to decide how I feel about that.

We have the weekend off. We are going away for some peace and solitude. I'm looking forward to that!

New Year's Eve
December 31st, 1978

Hey Diary - it's been another great year for me. The Navy is still the best job ever! I'm taking some creative writing classes for fun, as well as some pre-requisite classes at Howard University to prepare for a master's degree program in counseling. Since I transfer next year, I won't start my degree until I know where I'm transferring to.

Scotty and I are doing okay. Good days and not so good days. He's been very moody and I've been concentrating on my work and classes. I've been going to church off and on. I haven't decided if I want to settle in a church, just sort of church hopping. It's okay. Civilians think differently than military people and church people think differently than anybody. I don't know if I'm ready to deal with their mindset about life in general and especially about the military. More importantly, I'm not ready to deal with how they will view me, why I left the church, what I've been doing and who I've been doing it with. I just don't want to be bothered with nosey, hypercritical Christians who pretend they never had sex before or smoked a joint or sipped on some cognac or Boones Farm; whichever they preferred. I just don't want to be bothered. Whenever I go, I sit in the back, leave before the appeal and before the hugs followed by, "Come to our house for lunch!" UGH! Give me a break!

Valentine's Day,

February 14th, 1979

Diary - Scotty had a really rough week, so I decided I would treat him to a massage. He enjoyed it. We went out to dinner. He keeps ruining our nights out bringing up our upcoming transfers. He said he has started negotiating orders which caught me off guard, because we had decided we would discuss our options before we negotiated transfer orders. I asked him why would he negotiate orders without us discussing it. He said something extremely out of the blue. He "suggested" I should get out of the Navy and follow him to his next duty station. That way I could go to school and not have to worry about my credits and we would be together. I asked him what did he mean, "be together?" He said, "You know, like we are now?"

I just looked at him. I did not say a word because my brain was telling me to ask him had he lost his "ever-loving-sweet-mind!" But, I didn't say anything...right away. My mind is whirling...

"What would make him think I want to get out of the navy...ever...especially, when he knows I plan to stay for 30 years?"

"What part of him does he think is so great to make me want to get out of the Navy and follow him around, with or without benefit of marriage?"

"What made him think I would want to "live" with him — we don't live together now?"

"Why would I leave a perfectly good career I love with excellent benefits and perks, to follow a man that says he loves me, but don't want to marry me?"

"Why would I want to do that!?"

My brain is SCREAMING!

After a long silence, I asked him would he consider following me around, and be together "just like we are now?" Immediately, without hesitation or a pause to reflect on the question, he said, "Of course not!" He even had the nerve to have an attitude attached to his response as if he were thinking, "Have YOU lost your mind?!"

I stood up and asked him to please take me home. When we got to my house, I got out of his car, asked him to go home and I'd talk to him another day. I walked into my house and closed the door. One more second in his presence and he would not have made it to law school and I would have caught a charge. "Honestly, has he lost his mind?" "HELP ME GOD!" And now, there are tears. I would love to say these are "love-hurting" tears, but, they are not. These are "I'm-so-mad-I-could-spit!" tears.

CHAPTER SIX

September 14th, 1999

2:30 P.M.

We had several open cases, plus this newest one from the sailor's mother, so we were busy. Before I knew it, it was 2:30 P.M. and we had an even more hectic afternoon. The last walk-in just left. I took off my jacket and my shoes and sat down, trying to remember if I had eaten lunch. No lunch and no time for a snack because in an hour I have one more meeting with someone from the U. S. Navy Atlantic Fleet headquarters office in Norfolk, Virginia concerning the case onboard the USS GREENWOOD LAKE. I wanted to get some notes together before the meeting started. It is highly unusual for a case like this to become a congressional matter; they are usually handled at the local level. Also, it is highly unusual for us to meet with anyone concerning these cases this early in the investigation. This entire case is very peculiar. I would think they were trying to circumvent the system or hide something. I hope they don't think they can cover up anything. I will find out what the truth is. The reason I am so good at my job and why Congresswoman Abraham hired me is because I'm a suspicious, dogmatic and consistently thorough investigator. She knows the struggle I had (still having) with my own faith which is why she trusts me to make sure this young sailor's rights are not being violated. I admire, that at such a young age, he knows that he wants to serve God and his country, but that his relationship with God comes first. There is so much controversy, even in this century of equal opportunity, with regard to religious liberty. Unlike this young man, my struggle was not with my superiors or my co-workers. My struggle was with myself. It took me a while to decide I really wanted a relationship with God and when I did, I fell in love with a Man that was not trying to get under my skirt (as my grandmother used to say) but into my heart and spirit. Don't get me wrong, even now after all of these years, I still struggle...real Christians do. I just try not to worry, like most people do. When I was younger I didn't understand that God and worry didn't go together. I didn't understand that God cared about my big and my little issues. I'm glad I understand it now...My God's got BIG shoulders.

April 5th, 1979

Dear Diary - Scotty and I have managed somehow to reach our second anniversary, but we are not doing well right now. He's having issues that he has to work out for himself; issues I had to realize I can't help him with. In psychology class I'm learning a lot about myself and how to deal with other people. He is upset because I won't agree to end my career to further his, despite the fact that he has no intention of marrying me. He's traveling more and when he is in town he pouts because my time includes both work and personal events, other than him, that make my life complete. He's being a baby. Unfortunate for him, I'm not the mothering type. He works, I work...he goes to school - I go to school...he has his friends and I have my friends. Right now, as far as I'm concerned, the time we manage to have right now is enough.

What he really hates is that I've added church, on Saturday, to my list of things to do. He knows that I have been making it a point to go to church, not every week, but more often than before. Until I started going back to church, he wasn't available to me most Saturday mornings. Gym, drill, out of town, sleep…whatever. Now that I have something to do and may not be available to him, he's having tantrums. He'll live.

During my church hopping escapades I found a small church I really like. There are people my age and military families there, someone that speaks my language. WooHoo!

I told Scotty several weeks ago about a dinner-theater event at the church on Saturday and it would be nice if we went together. Lately, very seldom are we both in town on the weekend together. I wanted us to spend it together and so did he, but doing two entirely different things. He wasn't interested and actually refused to go with me to the play; and, he had an attitude because I went without him. I had already bought the tickets, so I asked my friend to go with me. It was a great play and the food was delicious; he missed out. Actually, I didn't hear from him the entire weekend so I spent time with my friends. He called around five yesterday, but I was studying for an exam and told him I couldn't be with him. He's upset but he'll get over it. He wants me to be at his beck and call when it's convenient for him, but I won't allow him to manipulate my time nor my life. I can't let him think my entire life revolves around him alone; because he definitely doesn't allow his life to revolve around me. Very seldom, these days, is he available when I want or need him.

If he is going to have drama because I go to church, or because I refuse to leave my career, then he has issues I'm not about to deal with.

October 30th, 1979

Diary - I'm glad Scotty has gotten over himself, but I know we are slowing down. Maybe that's a good thing. Maybe our time is coming to an end.

Actually, I have been using my time rediscovering my relationship with Christ. The church has a great choir and a "decent" preacher (he's kinda old). The fellowship makes up for the preacher.

I have been struggling with my relationship with Scotty and he is struggling with my relationship with Christ. I love Scotty but my relationship with Jesus will prove to have long term benefits that Scotty cannot provide for me, even if he wanted to. Unfortunately, ever since I decided to make this commitment to Jesus, Scotty refuses to understand how important it is to me. He hates that almost every Sabbath I'm at church; he hates I'm not clubbing with him, even though in the last two years I could count on two fingers how often we went to the club; clubbing was NEVER our thing. Why now, all of a sudden, he wants to frequent the club? HUH! He hates that I've been sorta-kinda limiting our "physical activities." I pray every day and night because it's hard to tell Scotty "no not today" and there are days when I can't resist... I don't even try. I'm glad I know God is faithful even when I am not.

Scotty hates that he is no longer my "all-in-all." Deep down he knows I'm not getting out of the Navy for him and I'm sure he hates my new lifestyle. One day he asked me, "How can you want to spend more time with Jesus and that church, than me?" I just looked at him; even he knew that was an idiot question. Ha! Ha! Once again, he'll be alright.

CHAPTER 7

September 14th, 1999

3:15 P.M.

As my assistant, part of Nancy's job is to do most of the research on the ship and the personnel involved. We locate as much data as possible to draw a picture of what the atmosphere of the ship is and also information concerning the practices of the current commanding officer when dealing with equal employment or harassment issues. We also find out as much as we can about the military member and family lifestyle. Sometimes we find enough relevant information and sometimes we don't. After this phase is complete, we then send a formal Letter of Congressional Inquiry to the command. For some reason someone wants to give me their side of the story before I'm ready to hear it. This is very suspicious indeed.

In the back of my mind, I seem to remember a previous incident with the USS GREENWOOD LAKE, not with a

Georgia constituent, but a discrimination complaint involving a service member from Louisiana. I made myself a note to investigate this further. I wonder if the same commanding officer is involved.

I am standing in the archives library, looking up background information on the ship and the commanding officer. In order for me to reach the top shelf, I have to use a footstool. The cabinet was built by and for Paul Bunyan. I'm standing on this stool, sleeveless, in my stocking feet, when Nancy comes to the door of the file room and says in a very puzzling tone, "Nat, Commander Scott is here — 30 minutes early." I almost fell trying to turn to look at her. "You say what now? Commander Who?!" I stepped off of the stool and stood there because my head was a little dizzy. I just looked at her as she said, "Commander Scott, from the Navy JAG office. He is your 3:45 appointment." As is my habit, I took a deep breath, shook my head to clear the air and said to Nancy, "I'm sure there are at least a thousand Commander Scott's working for Navy JAG, there is NO WAY he is "my"

Commander Scott who happens to work for Navy JAG".

Nancy is smiling at me the way she does when she knows I'm

trying to convince myself of something that I know is impossible

but true. She laughed and she said, "Your Commander

Scott?" I said, "YOU know what I mean. No time for

funnies!" She smiled, and then asked, "What do you want me

to do with him?" My bad angel chimed in immediately.

"Throw him out the window!" My good angel reminded me

(again) that Christians don't think such thoughts and besides,

Nancy is too short to complete such a task.

     I had to walk out of the library and through the visitor

waiting area without my jacket, in my stocking feet, because

they were in my office. When I walked into the waiting room

my knees became a little weak. I held on to the door so that I

would not look as if I was unstable. There may be a thousand

Commander Scotts, but there is only one that looks like him...

standing, sitting it doesn't matter. He was sitting on the coach

looking through a Message Magazine, which is ironic because

I'm sure he remembers it from back in the day. I was trying

not to have an attitude with God, but I just did not understand what type of divine tactic this was.

"God, what is going on here?" "Why is he here!?"

"Did he know this morning that he would be meeting with me?"

"Did *YOU* know he was coming here...? Of course, You knew!" "Why is he here?!"

I just need you to tell me *WHY* is he here and *WHAT* am I supposed to do now!"

"*YOU KNOW WHAT HE DID!*"

November 3rd, 1979

Diary - the weekend was horrible. Scotty ruined both of our birthdays. First, he was very late picking me up on Thursday, so I was in a bad mood. But, I wanted to have a good, relaxing time so I pulled myself together. On Friday he told me he chose orders and that he was transferring early. He refused to understand why this news was disturbing to me and then he had the nerve to say that he assumed I would get out and come with him like he suggested. I walked out of the room because I was so overwhelmed with anger and I did not want him to confuse my angry tears for love-hurt tears. I didn't want to talk or yell at him...or worst push him out the window. I walked along the beach for about an hour. I don't remember being this upset the entire time I've known him. He just totally disregarded my career or my desires for what I want in my life... including whether I still wanted him.

After about an hour I went back to the room. Of course, he wasn't there. When he came back, I asked him why he thought my career was not important to the point that I should quit to follow him and his career and depend on him without benefit of marriage. He said, "Nattie my career, as a lawyer is more stable and more important than your career as a records keeper in the Navy and no I don't want to get married, we can just live together." I couldn't help but remind him, "You have not taken one law class, so, classifying yourself as a lawyer was a little presumptuous. Also, we barely get along living in separate apartments, what makes you think we can get along in one apartment? But most importantly, what makes you think I would consider living with you unmarried?" He rolled his eyes and said something smart about my church under his breath. I did not pursue. I refuse to fight with him. I slept on the couch.

We tried to have a pleasant weekend, but it was pretty much ruined. We didn't argue, but we didn't have much love for each other either. We checked out on Sunday and drove back home, pretty much in silence. He dropped me off and left, which was fine because I needed to not look at him another minute. More tears...UGH!

New Year's Eve
December 31ˢᵗ, 1979

"Diary - Scotty and I are done. He came by yesterday." I thought we were going to plan our New Year's Eve Day celebration, instead, he told me that he was transferring next week. I just looked at him. For two and a half years we were inseparable. He would hold me as if no one else would fit in his arms. He said he would never let me go.

And when I asked him how he could throw us away so calmly, he said that he gave me what he considered to be a viable solution, but I was being stubborn and he had to consider his career over us. In other words, "us" is not as important to him as his career. His exact words were "It's not that I don't love you, Nattie, but how could I pass up this once in a career opportunity...for what, marriage and an enlisted paycheck for the rest of my life? No thank you!" My response to him as I moved towards the door was, "In other words..." he cut me off before I could finish my sentence, "My love for you is not bigger than my career and my goals for myself. As much as I love you, this is business. Love won't make me successful — I'm sure you can understand that, Nattie." "And my career, my education or my love for you, Scotty, has no importance to you at all, right?" With this strangely sad look on his face he replied, "I'm sorry Nattie." And he walked out and I closed the door.

Uninvited Memories

You know what Diary - I have no tears left for him. Tomorrow begins a new year and the beginning of a new life for me. Talk to you tomorrow. Good night.

CHAPTER EIGHT

September 14th, 1999

3:15 P.M.

"Commander Scott." As the words trailed from my lips he looked up in utter disbelief. At that moment I realized he did not know he was meeting with me.

"Nattie?" It seems he was just as confused as I was. "I was told I would be meeting with Dr. Morgan. I didn't realize it was you — your name changed?" Then he looked at my feet and said, "I see you still don't like shoes!" I said, "What can I say...please excuse me, I will be with you in a moment."

I went into my office and closed the door while Nancy went to collect my notes from the library. I sat there for a moment asking for guidance. God, please tell me "Why is he here?" Then it all became clear...Navy JAG in Atlanta...The USS GREENWOOD LAKE and the Navy JAG Office sent him here to meet with me. He is the liaison between us and them. He was sent here to lay out their side of the story. I'm sure he was very confident that he would be able to make his point without any resistance from my office. Now that he realizes he is meeting with me, I wonder what is going through his head. Is he still as cocky as he was all those years ago? Does he think I'm just as naïve as I was all those years ago?

I reached for my phone. "Nancy, would you please show the commander to the conference room." She responded, "Yes ma'am. Your notes are already on the table." I replied "No, put the notes on your desk, I'll get them in a moment." "Yes ma'am."

I stood up and put my shoes on. I looked in the mirror on the back of my door, checked my dress, jacket, my hair, pearls and lipstick. "You are Dr. Natalee Morgan and YOU are in charge." As I walked out of my office towards the conference room I prayed, "God please keep me professional and clear-minded for the sake of the young sailor onboard the USS GREENWOOD LAKE. You gave me this job so that

I can help him. Don't let my feelings and uninvited memories get in the way. In Jesus Name..." When I picked up my notes from Nancy's desk, with some concern in her voice she asked, "Nat will you be alright?" I took a deep breath as I replied, "Yes ma'am, but could you please bring me a cup of Earl Grey and him, coffee, cream no sugar?"

As I reached for the door knob to the conference room, I thought about the words he used as he walked out the door that night so long ago..."this is all about business, not personal."

As I walked in, he stood up. I reach out to shake his hand. "Commander Scott thank you for waiting. Please, sit. I see you are here to represent the USS GREENWOOD LAKE. What are your concerns?"

Made in the USA
Monee, IL
26 October 2021

80816321R00046